SERMONS AND SAYINGS

SERMONS AND SAYINGS

BY MEISTER ECKHART

translated into English by Claud Field

ISBN-13: 978-1-950330-01-0
WWW.BIGFONTBOOKS.COM

Contents

The Attractive Power of God

ST JOHN vi. 44.—"No one can come unto Me, except the Father which hath sent Me draw him."

OUR Lord Jesus Christ hath in the Gospel spoken with His own blessed lips these words, which signify, "No man can come to Me unless My Father draw him." In another place He says, "I am in the Father and the Father in Me." Therefore whoever cometh to the Son cometh to the Father. Further, He saith, "I and the Father are One. Therefore whomsoever the Father draweth, the Son draweth likewise." St Augustine also saith, "The works of the Holy Trinity are insepa-rable from each other." Therefore the Father draweth to the Son, and the Son draweth to the Holy Ghost, and the Holy Ghost draweth to the Father and the Son; and each Person of the Trinity, when He draweth to the Two Others, draweth to Himself, because the Three are One. The Father draweth with the might of His power, the Son draweth with His unfathomable wisdom, the Holy Ghost draweth with His love. Thus we are drawn by the Sacred Trinity with the cords of Power,

Wisdom and Love, when we are drawn from an evil thing to a good thing, and from a good thing to a better, and from a better thing to the best of all. Now the Father draws us from the evil of sin to the goodness of His grace with the might of His measureless power, and He needs all the resources of His strength in order to convert sinners, more than when He was about to make heaven and earth, which He made with His own power without help from any creature. But when He is about to convert a sinner, He always needs the sinner's help. "He converts thee not without thy help," as St Augustine says.

Therefore deadly sin is a breach of nature, a death of the soul, a disquiet of the heart, a weakening of power, a blindness of the sense, a sorrow of the spirit, a death of grace, a death of virtue, a death of good works, an aberration of the spirit, a fellowship with the devil, an expulsion of Christianity, a dungeon of hell, a banquet of hell, an eternity of hell. Therefore, if thou committest a deadly sin thou art guilty of all these and incurrest their consequences. Regarding the first point: Deadly sin is a breach of nature, for every man's nature is an image and likeness and mirror of the Trinity, of Godhead and of eternity. All these together are marred by a deadly sin; therefore, it is a breach of nature. Such sin is also the death of the soul, for death is to lose life. Now God is the life of the soul, and deadly sin separates from God; therefore it is a death of the soul. Deadly sin is also a disquiet of the heart, for everything rests nowhere except in its own proper place; and the proper resting-place of the soul is nowhere except in God as St Augustine saith, "Lord! Thou hast made us for Thyself, therefore we may not rest anywhere save in Thee." Deadly sin is also a weakening of the powers, for by his own power no one can throw off the load of sin nor restrain himself from committing sin. It is also a blindness of the sense, for it prevents a man recognizing how brief is the space of time that can be spent in the pleasure of voluptuousness, and how long are the pains of hell and the joys of heaven. Deadly sin is also a death of all grace, for whenever such a sin is committed, the soul is bereft of all grace. Similarly, it is the death of all virtue and good works, and an aberration of the spirit.

It is also a fellowship with the Devil, for everything hath fellowship with its like; and sin maketh the soul and Satan resemble each other. It is also an expulsion of Christianity, for it depriveth the sinner of all the profit that comes from Christianity. It is also a dungeon of hell, for if the soul remain in the purity in which God created her, neither angel nor devil may rob her of her freedom. But sin confines it in hell. Sin is also an eternity of hell, for eternity is in the will, and were it not in the will, it would not be in the consciousness.

Now, people say when they commit sin, that they do not intend to do so always; they intend to turn away from sin. That is just as though a man were to kill himself and suppose that he could make himself alive again by his own strength. That is, however, impossible; but to turn from sin by one's own power and come to God is still much more impossible. Therefore, whosoever is to turn from sin and come to God in His heavenly kingdom, must be drawn by the heavenly Father with the might of His divine power. The Father also draws the Son who comes to help us with His grace, by stimulating our free will to turn away from, and hate sin, which has drawn us aside from God, and from the immutable goodness of the Godhead. Then, if she is willing, He pours the gift of His grace into the soul, which renounces all her misery and sin, and all her works become living. Now, this grace springs from the centre of Godhead and the Father's heart, and flows perpetually, nor ever ceases, if the soul obeys His everlasting love. Therefore He saith in the prophets: "I have loved thee with an everlasting love, therefore with loving kindness have I drawn thee." Out of the overflow of His universal love He desires to draw all to Himself, and to His Only-begotten Son, and to the Holy Ghost in the joy of the heavenly kingdom. Now, we should know that before our Lord Jesus Christ was born, the Heavenly Father drew men with all His might for five thousand, two hundred years; and yet, as far as we know, brought not one into the heavenly kingdom. So, when the Son saw that the Father had thus strongly drawn men and even wearied Himself, and yet not succeeded, He said to the Father: "I will draw them with the cords of a man." It was as though He said, "I see well, Father, that Thou with all Thy might, canst not succeed, therefore will I myself draw them with the cords of a man."

Therefore the Son came down from heaven, and was incarnate of a Virgin, and took upon Him all our bodily weaknesses, except sin and folly, into which Adam had cast us; and out of all His words and works and limbs and nerves, He made a cord, and drew us so skillfully, and so heartily, that the bloody sweat poured from His sacred Body. And when He had drawn men without ceasing for three and thirty years, He saw the beginnings of a movement and the redemption of all things that would follow. Therefore He said, "And I, if I be lifted up on the Cross, will draw all men unto Me." Therefore He was stretched upon the Cross, and laid aside all His glory, and whatever might hinder His drawing men.

Now, there are three natural means of attraction with which Christ on the Cross drew to Himself between the third and the ninth hour, more people than He had drawn before during the three and thirty years of His life. The first means by which He draws is affinity, that affinity which brings creatures of the same species together, and like to its like. With this cord of affinity he drew men to the Godhead, Whom He always resembles. In order that God may draw more to Himself, and forget His wrath, the Son saith, "Beloved Father, seeing that Thou wouldest not forgive sins because of all the former sacrifices offered, lo I, Thine Only begotten Son, Who resemble Thy Godhead in all things, in Whom Thou hast hidden all the riches of divine love, I come to the Cross, that I may be a living sacrifice before Thine eyes; that out of Thy fatherly compassion Thou mayest bend and look on Me, Thine only Son, and on My Blood flowing from My wounds, and slake the fiery sword with which in the angel's hands Thou hast barred the way to Paradise, that all who have repented and bewailed their sins through Me, may enter therein."

The second means of attraction which He used is Emptiness, as we see when we place one end of a hollow pipe in water, and draw up it by suction; the water runs up the stem to the mouth, because the emptiness of the pipe, from which the air has been drawn, draws the water to itself. So Our Lord Jesus Christ made Himself empty that He might wisely draw all things to Himself. Therefore He let all the blood that was in His Body flow out, and so attracted to Himself all the compassion and grace that was in His Father's heart, so completely and profitably as to suffice for the whole world. Accordingly, the Father said, "My compassion will I never forget," and further, "Now, My Son, be bold and strong that Thou mayest lead the people altogether into the land which I have promised, the land of heavenly joys, the land which floweth with the honey of My Godhead, and with the milk of Thy manhood."

The third means of attraction is this—that as we see the sun draw up the mists from the earth to heaven, so the heart of our Lord Jesus Christ waxed hot as a fiery furnace upon the Cross, so fiercely burned the flame of love which He felt towards the whole world. Thus, with the heat of His love, from which nothing could be hidden, so intense was it—He drew the whole world to Himself. Never did our Lord Jesus Christ display such great love as when He suffered the torture of the Cross when He gave His life for us, and washed our sins with His precious Blood. Therefore with the cords of Love, He drew us all to Himself upon the Cross that those who feel the drawing of His death and martyrdom might live with Him in everlasting felicity.

Now when the Holy Spirit saw that the Only Begotten Son of the Father had drawn so wisely that He had won to Himself all things in heaven and earth, He also felt impelled by His own love and kindness to draw. Therefore He said, "I will also draw with My cords and My net." So He made a net of the seven high attributes of the Father, of the seven graces of the Son, of His own seven gifts, and of the seven Christian virtues. Thus He assures us that we shall never perish, for we are so caught by His goodness that He expels from us all the evil works of the flesh, and produces in us His fruits, so that we gain the reward of everlasting life. May the Father of His love, and the Son of His grace, and the Holy Spirit with His fellowship, grant us to be worthy of the same. Amen.

The eye with which I see God is the same eye with which God sees me.
- Meister Eckhart

The Nearness of the Kingdom

ST LUKE xxi, 31.—" Know that the Kingdom of God is near."

OUR Lord saith that the Kingdom of God is near us. Yea, the Kingdom of God is within us as St Paul saith "our salvation is nearer than when we believed." Now we should know in what manner the Kingdom of God is near us. Therefore let us pay diligent attention to the meaning of the words. If I were a king, and did not know it, I should not really be a king. But, if I were fully convinced that I was a king, and all mankind coincided in my belief, and I knew that they shared my conviction, I should indeed be a king, and all the wealth of the king would be mine. But, if one of these three conditions were lacking, I should not really be a king.

In similar fashion our salvation depends upon our knowing and recognizing the Chief Good which is God Himself. I have a capacity in my soul for taking in God entirely. I am as sure as I live that nothing is so near to me as God. God is nearer to me than I am to myself;

my existence depends on the nearness and presence of God. He is also near things of wood and stone, but they know it not. If a piece of wood became as aware of the nearness of God as an archangel is, the piece of wood would be as happy as an archangel. For this reason man is happier than the inanimate wood, because he knows and understands how God is near him. His happiness increases and diminishes in proportion to the increase and diminution in his knowledge of this. His happiness does not arise from this that God is near him, and in him, and that He possesses God; but from this, that he knows the nearness of God, and loves Him, and is aware that "the Kingdom of God is near." So, when I think on God's Kingdom, I am compelled to be silent because of its immensity, because God's Kingdom is none other than God Himself with all His riches. God's Kingdom is no small thing: we may survey in imagination all the worlds of God's creation, but they are not God's Kingdom. In whichever soul God's Kingdom appeareth, and which knoweth God's Kingdom, that soul needeth no human preaching or instruction; it is taught from within and assured of eternal life. Whoever knows and recognizes how near God's Kingdom is to him may say with Jacob, "God is in this place, and I knew it not."

God is equally near in all creatures. The wise man saith, "God hath spread out His net over all creatures, so that whosoever wishes to discover Him may find and recognize Him in each one." Another saith, "He knows God rightly who recognizes Him alike in all things." To serve God with fear is good; to serve Him out of love is better; but to fear and love Him together is best of all. To have a restful or peaceful life in God is good; to bear a life of pain in patience is better; but to have peace in the midst of pain is the best of all.

A man may go into the field and say his prayer and be aware of God, or, he may be in Church and be aware of God; but, if he is more aware of Him because he is in a quiet place, that is his own deficiency and not due to God, Who is alike present in all things and places, and is willing to give Himself everywhere so far as lies in Him. He knows God rightly who knows Him everywhere. St Bernard saith, "How is it that mine eye and not my foot sees heaven? Because mine eye is more like heaven than my foot is. So, if my soul is to know God, it must be God-like."

Now, how is the soul to arrive at this heavenly state that it recognizes God in itself, and knows that He is near? By copying the heavens, which can receive no impulse from without to mar their tranquility. Thus must the soul, which would know God, be rooted and grounded in Him so steadfastly, as to suffer no perturbation of fear or hope, or joy or sorrow, or love or hate, or anything which may disturb its peace.

The heavens are everywhere alike remote from earth, so should the soul be remote from all earthly things alike so as not to be nearer to one than another. It should keep the same attitude of aloofness in love and hate, in possession and renouncement, that is, it should be simultaneously dead, resigned and lifted up. The heavens are pure and clear without shadow of stain, out of space and out of time. Nothing corporeal is found there. Their revolutions are incredibly swift and independent of time, though time depends on them. Nothing hinders the soul so much in attaining to the knowledge of God as time and place. Therefore, if the soul is to know God, it must know Him outside time and place, since God is neither in this or that, but One and above them. If the soul is to see God, it must look at nothing in time; for while the soul is occupied with time or place or any image of the kind, it cannot recognize

God. If it is to know Him, it must have no fellowship with nothingness. Only he knows God who recognizes that all creatures are nothingness. For, if one creature be set over against another, it may appear to be beautiful and somewhat, but if it be set over against God, it is nothing. I say moreover: If the soul is to know God it must forget itself and lose itself, for as long as it contemplates self, it cannot contemplate God. When it has lost itself and everything in God, it finds itself again in God when it attains to the knowledge of Him, and it finds also everything which it had abandoned complete in God. If I am to know the highest good, and the everlasting Godhead, truly, I must know them as they are in themselves apart from creation. If I am to know real existence, I must know it as it is in itself, not as it is parceled out in creatures.

The whole Being of God is contained in God alone. The whole of humanity is not contained in one man, for one man is not all men. But in God the soul knows all humanity, and all things at their highest level of existence, since it knows them in their essence. Suppose any one to be in a beautifully adorned house: he would know much more about it than one who had never entered therein, and yet wished to speak much about it. Thus, I am as sure, as I am of my own existence and God's, that, if the soul is to know God, it must know Him outside of time and place. Such a soul will know clearly how near God's kingdom is.

Schoolmen have often asked how it is possible for the soul to know God. It is not from severity that God demands much from men in order to obtain the knowledge of Himself: it is of His kindness that He wills the soul by effort to grow capacious of receiving much, and that He may give much. Let no man think that to attain this knowledge is too difficult, although it may sound so, and indeed the commencement of it, and the renouncement of all things, is difficult. But when one attains to it, no life is easier nor more pleasant nor more lovable, since God is always endeavouring to dwell with man, and teach him in order to bring him to Himself. No man desires anything so eagerly as God desires to bring men to the knowledge of Himself. God is always ready, but we are very unready. God is near us, but we are far from Him. God is within, and we are without. God is friendly; we are estranged. The prophet saith, "God leadeth the righteous by a narrow path into a broad and wide place, that is into the true freedom of those who have become one spirit with God." May God help us all to follow Him that He may bring us to Himself. Amen.

Man goes far away or near but God never goes far-off; he is always standing close at hand, and even if he cannot stay within he goes no further than the door.
- Meister Eckhart

The Angel's Greeting

ST. LUKE i. 28.—"Hail, thou that art highly favoured among women, the Lord is with thee."

HERE there are three things to understand: the first, the modesty of the angel; the second, that he thought himself unworthy to accost the Mother of God; the third, that he not only addressed her, but the great multitude of souls who long after God.

I affirm that had the Virgin not first borne God spiritually He would never have been born from her in bodily fashion. A certain woman said to Christ, "Blessed is the womb that bear Thee." To which Christ answered, "Nay, rather blessed are they that hear the Word of God and keep it." It is more worthy of God that He be born spiritually of every pure and virgin soul, than that He be born of Mary. Hereby we should understand that humanity is, so to speak, the Son of God born from all eternity. The Father produced all creatures, and me among them, and I issued forth from Him with all creatures, and yet I abide in the Father. Just as the word which I now speak is conceived and spoken forth by me, and you all receive it, yet none the less it abides in me. Thus I and all creatures abide in the Father.

Hereto I adjoin a parable. There were a certain man and wife; the woman by accident lost an eye, and was sorely troubled thereat. Her husband then said to her, "Wife, why are you troubled? "She answered, "It is not the loss of my eye that troubles me, but the thought that you may love me less on account of that loss." He said, "I love you all the same." Not long after he put one of his own eyes out, and came to his wife and said, "Wife, that you may believe I love you, I have made myself like you: I, too, now, have only one eye." So men could hardly believe that God loved them till God put one of His eyes out, that is took upon Himself human nature, and was made man. Just as fire infuses its essence and clearness into the dry wood, so has God done with man. He has created the human soul and infused His glory into it, and yet in His own essence has remained unchangeable. If you ask me whether, seeing that my spiritual birth is out of time, whether I am an eternal son, I answer "Yes," and "No." In the everlasting foreknowledge of God, I slumbered like a word unspoken. He hath brought me forth

His son in the image of His eternal father-hood, that I also should be a father and bring forth Him. It is as if one stood before a high mountain, and cried, "Art thou there?" The echo comes back, "Art thou there?" If one cries, "Come out." the echo answers, "Come out."

Again: If I am in a higher place and say to some one, "Come up hither," that might be difficult for him. But if I say, "Sit down," that would be easy. Thus God dealeth with us. When man humbles himself, God cannot restrain His mercy; He must come down and pour His grace into the humble man, and He gives Himself most of all, and all at once, to the least of all. It is essential to God to give, for His essence is His goodness and His goodness is His love. Love is the root of all joy and sorrow. Slavish fear of God is to be put away. The right fear is the fear of losing God. If the earth flee downward from heaven, it finds heaven beneath it; if it flee upward, it comes again to heaven. The earth cannot flee from heaven: whether it flee up or down, the heaven rains its influence upon it, and stamps its impress upon it, and makes it fruitful, whether it be willing or not. Thus doth God with men: whoever thinketh to escape Him, flies into His bosom, for every corner is open to Him. God brings forth His Son in thee, whether thou likest it or not, whether thou sleepest or wakest; God worketh His own will. That man is unaware of it, is man's fault, for his taste is so spoilt by feeding on earthly things that he cannot relish God's love. If we had love to God, we should relish God, and all His works; we should receive all things from God, and work the same works as He worketh.

God created the soul after the image of His highest perfection. He issued forth from the treasure-house of the everlasting Fatherhood in which He had rested from all eternity. Then the Son opened the tent of His everlasting glory and came forth from His high place to fetch His Bride, whom the Father had espoused to Him from all Eternity, back to that heaven from which she came. Therefore He came forth rejoicing as a bridegroom and suffered the pangs of love. Then He returned to His secret chamber in the silence and stillness of the everlasting Fatherhood. As He came forth from the Highest, so He returned to the Highest with His Bride, and revealed to her the hidden treasures of His Godhead.

The first beginning is for the sake of the last end. God Himself doth not rest because He is the beginning, but because He is the end and goal of all creation. This end is concealed in the darkness of the everlasting Godhead, and is unknown, and never was known, and never will be known. God Himself remains unknown; the light of the everlasting Father shineth in darkness, and the darkness comprehended it not. May the truth of which we have spoken lead us to the truth. Amen.

A just person is one who is conformed and transformed into justice.
- Meister Eckhart

True Hearing

ECCLESIASTICUS xxiv. 30.—"Whoso heareth Me shall not be confounded."

THE everlasting and paternal wisdom saith, "Whoso heareth Me is not ashamed." If he is ashamed of anything he is ashamed of being ashamed. Whoso worketh in Me sineth not. Whoso confesseth Me and feareth Me, shall have eternal life. Whoso will hear the wisdom of the Father must dwell deep, and abide at home, and be at unity with himself. Three things hinder us from hearing the everlasting Word. The first is fleshliness, the second is distraction, the third is the illusion of time. If a man could get free of these, he would dwell in eternity, and in the spirit, and in solitude, and in the desert, and there would hear the everlasting Word. Our Lord saith, "No man can hear My word nor my teaching without renouncing himself." All that the Eternal Father teaches and reveals is His being, His nature, and His Godhead, which He manifests to us in His Son, and teaches us that we are also His Son.

All that God worketh and teacheth, He worketh in His Son. All His work is directed to this end that we also may be His Son. When God sees that we are indeed His son, He yearns after us, and in the depth of His Divine Being waves of longing break forth, to reveal to us the abyss of His Godhead, and the fullness of His essence; He hastens to identify Himself with us. Herein He hath joy and gladness in full measure. God loveth men not less than He loveth Himself. If thou really lovest thyself, thou lovest all men as thyself; as long as thou lovest any one less than thyself, thou dost not really love thyself. That man is right who loves all men as himself.

Some folk say: "I love my friends, who do me kindness, more than other people." Such love is imperfect and incomplete; it is like having your sails only half-tilled with wind. When I love anyone as much as myself, I would just as soon that joy or sorrow, death or life were mine, as well as his. That would be the dictate of right reason.

St Paul felt such love when he said, "I would that I were cut off from God for my friends' sake." Now to be cut off from God is equivalent to suffering the pains of hell. Some ask whether St Paul was on the way to perfection or was perfect. I answer, he was perfect, or he would have spoken otherwise.

I wish further to elucidate this saying of St Paul that he was willing to be cut off from God. The highest act of renunciation for man is for God's sake to give up God, and that is what St Paul was willing to do; to give up all the blessings that he might receive from God. When for God's sake he gave up God, God still remained with him, since God's essence is Himself, not any impression or reception of Himself. He who does so is a true man to whom no grief may happen, any more than it happens to the Divine Being. There is a somewhat in the soul that is, as it were, a blood-relative of God. It is one, it has nothing in common with nothing, nor is it like nothingness, nothing. All that is created is nothing, all far from and foreign to the soul. Could I but find myself one instant in that sphere of pure existence, I should regard myself as little as a worm.

A question arises regarding the angels who dwell with us, serve us and protect us, whether their joys are equal to those of the angels in heaven, or whether they are diminished by the fact that they protect and serve us. No, they are certainly not; for the work of the angels is the will of God, and the will of God is the work of the angels; their service to us does not hinder their joy nor their working. If God told an angel to go to a tree and pluck caterpillars off it, the angel would be quite ready to do so, and it would be his happiness, if it were the will of God.

The man who abides in the will of God wills nothing else than what God is, and what He wills. If he were ill he would not wish to be well. If he really abides in God's will, all pain is to him a joy, all complication, simple: yea, even the pains of hell would be a joy to him. He is free and gone out from himself, and from all that he receives, he must be free. If my eye is to discern colour, it must itself be free from all colour. The eye with which I see God is the same with which God sees me. My eye and God's eye is one eye, and one sight, and one knowledge, and one love.

The man who abides in God's love must be dead to himself and all created things, and regard himself as a mere unit among a thousand million. Such a man must renounce himself and all the world. Supposing a man possessed all the world, and gave it back to God intact just as he received it, God would give him back, all the world and everlasting life to boot. And supposing there were another man who had nothing but a good will, and he thought in his heart, "Lord, were all this world mine, and two worlds more beside it, I would give them and myself also back to Thee as I received them from thee"; to that man God would give back as much as he had given away. And supposing a man had renounced himself for twenty years, if he took himself back for a moment, that man's renunciation would be as nothing. The man who has truly renounced himself and does not once cast a glance on what he has renounced, and thus remains immovable and unalterable, that man alone has really renounced self. May God and the Eternal Wisdom grant us to remain equally immovable and unalterable with Himself. Amen.

Only the hand that erases can write the true thing.
- Meister Eckhart

The knower and the known are one.
Simple people imagine that they should see God as if he stood there and they here.
This is not so.
God and I, we are one in knowledge.
- Meister Eckhart

The Self-Communication of God

ST JOHN xiv. 23.—"If a man love me, he will keep my words; and my Father will love him, and we will come unto him, and make our abode with him."

WE read in the Gospels that Our Lord fed many people with five loaves and two fishes. Speaking parabolically, we may say that the first loaf was— that we should know ourselves, what we have been everlastingly to God, and what we now are to Him. The second— that we should pity our fellow Christian who is blinded; his loss should grieve us as much as our own. The third— that we should know our Lord Jesus Christ's life, and follow it to the utmost of our capacity. The fourth— that we should know the judgments of God. All that may be said of the pains of hell is true. St Dionysius saith, "To be separated from God is hell, and the sight of God's countenance is heaven." The fifth is— that we should know the Godhead which has flowed into the Father and filled Him with joy, and which has flowed into the Son and filled Him with wisdom, and the Two are essentially one. Therefore said

Christ, "Where I am, there is My Father, and where My Father is, there am I" And They have flowed into the Holy Ghost and filled Him with good will. Therefore said Christ, "I and My Father have one Spirit," and the Holy Ghost has flowed into the soul.

The soul has by nature two capacities. The one is intelligence, which may comprehend the Holy Trinity with all its works and be contained by It as water is by a vessel. When the vessel is full, it has enclosed all that is contained in it, and is united with that which it has enclosed, and of which it is full. Thus intelligence becomes one with that which it has understood and comprehended. It is united therewith by grace, as the Son is one with the Father.

The second capacity is Will. That is a nobler one, and its essential characteristic is to plunge into the Unknown which is God. There the Will lays hold of God in a mysterious manner, and the Unknown God imparts His impress to the Will. The Will draws thought and all the powers of the soul after it in its train, so that the soul becomes one with God by grace, as the Holy Ghost is one with the Father and with the Son by nature. In God it is more worthy to be loved, than it is in itself. Therefore St Augustine saith that the soul is greater by its love-giving power than by its life-giving power. If man might only abide in this union, and do all the works which have ever been done by creatures, he would be no other than God, if his higher powers so brought his lower powers under control, that he could only work God-like works. That however may not be, and man's highest faculty therefore contemplates God as best it can, and so influences his lower faculties that they can discern between Good and Evil.

Adam possessed that union with God which we have spoken of, and while he had it, his capacity contained the capacities of all creatures. The load-stone attracts the needle, and the needle receives the magnetic power, so that it can also attract other needles and draw them to the load-stone. But if one draws the first needle away, all the other needles come with it. Thus was it with Adam: when, in his highest capacity, he was separated from God all his capacities deteriorated. Thence came also discord and the clashing of oppugnant wills among the lower creation, and deterioration of their powers down to the lowest. It is necessary, therefore, for all the creatures which issued forth from God to co-operate earnestly with all their powers to form a Man who may again attain that union with God which Adam enjoyed before he fell, and who may again restore to the creatures their forfeited powers. This is fulfilled in Christ as He Himself said, "I, if I be lifted up, will draw all men unto Me." He means, if He is exalted in our knowledge, He will draw us unto Himself. In Him human nature grew divine, and thanked God and loved Him with immeasurable love. This also befits God that he loves human nature with so great love. I counsel you, sisters and brothers, that you grow in knowledge, and thank God, while you are in time, that He brought you out of non-existence to existence, and united you with the Divine Nature. But if the Divine Nature be beyond your comprehension, believe simply on Christ;Â follow His holy example and remain steadfast. Convert Jews, heathen, heretics, bad Christians, and all who do not enjoy your knowledge of God, and are still astray.

Now rejoice, all ye powers of my soul, that you are so united with God that no one may separate you from Him. I cannot fully praise nor love Him therefore must I die, and cast myself into the divine void, till I rise from non-existence to existence. If I should remain entombed in flesh till the judgment day and suffer the pains of hell, that would be for me a small thing to bear for my beloved Lord Jesus Christ, if I had the certainty at last of not being separated from Him. While I am here, He is in me; after this life, I am in Him. All things are therefore possible to me, if I am united to Him Who can do all things. Previously I could not distinguish whether we were divine by nature or by grace. Then came Jesus and enlightened me so that I recognized in the Divine Nature Three Persons, and that the Father was the Bringer-Forth of all things, as St James says, "every perfect gift cometh down from the Father of lights."

The Father and the Son have one Will, and that Will is the Holy Ghost, Who gives Himself to the soul so that the Divine Nature permeates the powers of the soul so that it can only do God-like works. Just as a spring, which perpetually flows and waters the roots of the flowers, so that the flowers bloom and receive their colours from the water of the spring, so the Godhead imparts Itself to the capacities of the soul that it may grow in the likeness of God. The more that the soul receives of the Divine Nature, the more it grows like It, and the closer becomes its union with God. It may arrive at such an intimate union that God at last draws it to

Himself altogether, so that there is no distinction left, in the soul's consciousness, between itself and God, though God still regards it as a creature. Wherefore let yourselves not be misled by the light of nature. The higher the degree of knowledge which the soul attains to in the light of grace, the darker seems to it the light of nature. If the soul would know the real truth it must examine itself, whether it has withdrawn from all things, whether it has lost itself, whether it loves God purely with His love and nothing of its own at the same time, so that it may not be separated from Him by anything, and whether God alone dwells in it. If it has lost itself, it is as when the Virgin Mary lost Christ. She sought Him for three days, and yet was sure that she would find Him. All the while Christ was in the highest class in the school of His Father, unconscious of His mother's seeking Him. Thus happens it to the noble soul which goes to God to school, and learns there what God is in His essence, and what He is in the Trinity, and what He is in man, and what is most acceptable to Him. St Augustine saith that the righteousness of God in the Godhead and in the Trinity and in all creatures is the source of the chief joy which is in heaven. God in human nature is a lamp of living light, and "the light shineth in darkness and the darkness comprehendeth it not." The darkness must ever more flee the light, as the night flees day. Thus the soul learns to know God's will. St Paul saith, "This is God's will, our sanctification." And this is our sanctification, to know what we were before time; what we are in time, and what we shall be after time. Thus the soul loses itself in these three, and recketh naught of the body, till it comes to it in the temple, and obeys it without murmuring. The Father is a revelation of the Godhead, the Son is an image and countenance of the Father, and the Holy Ghost is an effulgence of that countenance, and a mutual love between Them, and these properties They have always possessed in Themselves. The Three Persons have stooped out of pity down to human nature, and the Son became man, and was the most despised man on the earth, and suffered pain at the hands of the creatures whom He Himself created with the Father, through Whose will He became man. Thus was Christ till His death, and when He rose from the dead then was seen the most despised of all men united with the Godhead in the Person of Christ.

He who would be serene and pure needs but one thing, detachment.
- Meister Eckhart

If God gave the soul his whole creation she would not be filled thereby but only with himself.
- Meister Eckhart

Sanctification

ST Luke x. 42.—"One thing is needful."

I HAVE read many writings both of heathen philosophers and inspired prophets, ancient and modern, and have sought earnestly to discover what is the best and highest quality whereby man may approach most nearly to union with God, and whereby he may most resemble the ideal of himself which existed in God, before God created men. And after having thoroughly searched these writings as far as my reason may penetrate, I find no higher quality than sanctification or separation from all creatures. Therefore said our Lord to Martha, "One thing is necessary," as if to say, "whoso wishes to be untroubled and content, must have one thing, that is sanctification."

Various teachers have praised love greatly, as St Paul does, when he saith, "to whatever height I may attain, if I have not love, I am nothing." But I set sanctification even above love; in the first place because the best thing in love is that it compels me to love God. Now it is a greater thing that I compel God to come to me, than that I compel myself to go to God. Sanctification compels God to come to me, and I prove this as follows:—

Everything settles in its own appropriate place; now God's proper place is that of oneness and holiness; these come from sanctification; therefore God must of necessity give Himself to a sanctified heart.

In the second place I set sanctification above love, because love compels me to suffer all things for the sake of God; sanctification compels me to be the recipient of nothing but God; now, it is a higher state to be the recipient of nothing but God than to suffer all things for God, because in suffering one must have some regard to the person who inflicts the suffering, but sanctification is independent of all creatures.

Many teachers also praise humility as a virtue. But I set sanctification above humility for the following reason. Although humility may exist without sanctification, perfect sanctification cannot exist without perfect humility. Perfect humility tends to the annihilation of self; sanctification also is so close to self-annihilation that nothing can come between them. Therefore perfect sanctification cannot exist without humility, and to have both of these virtues is better than to have only one of them.

The second reason why I set sanctification above humility is that humility stoops to be under all creatures, and in doing so goes out of itself. But sanctification remains self-contained. But to remain contained within oneself is nobler than to go out of oneself for any purpose whatever; therefore saith the Psalmist, "The King's daughter is all glorious within," that is, all her glory is from her inwardness. Perfect sanctification has no inclination nor going-out towards any creature; it wishes neither to be above or below, neither to be like nor unlike any creature, but only to be one. Whosoever wishes to be this or that wishes to be somewhat; but sanctification wishes to be nothing.

But some one may say: "All virtues must have existed in fullness in Our Lady, therefore perfect sanctification must have been in her. If sanctification is higher than humility, why did Our Lady speak of her humility, and not of her sanctification, when she said, "For He hath regarded the lowliness of His handmaiden?" To this I answer that God possesses both sanctification and humility, so far as we may attribute virtues to God. Now thou shouldest know that His humility brought God to stoop down to human nature, and our Lady knew that He wished for the same quality in her, and in that matter had regard to her humility alone. Therefore she made mention of her humility and not of her sanctification, in which she remained unmoved and unaffected. If she had said, "He hath regarded the sanctification of His handmaiden," her sanctification would have been disturbed, for, so to speak, would have been a going out of herself. Therefore the Psalmist said, "I will hear what the Lord God will say in me," as if to say, "If God will Speak to me, let Him come in, for I will not come out." And Boethius saith, "Men, why seek ye outside you what is inside you— salvation?"

I set also sanctification above pity, for pity is only going out of oneself to sympathize with one's fellow-creature's sorrows. From such an out-going sanctification is free and abides in itself, and does not let itself be troubled. To speak briefly: when I consider all the virtues I find none so entirely without flaw and so conducive to union with God as sanctification.

The philosopher Avicenna says, "The spirit which is truly sanctified attains to so lofty a degree that all which it sees is real, all which it desires is granted, and in all which it commands, it is obeyed." When the free spirit is stablished in true sanctification, it draws God to itself, and were it placed beyond the reach of contingencies, it would assume the properties of God. But God cannot part with those to anyone; all that He can do for the sanctified spirit is to impart Himself to it. The man who is wholly sanctified is so drawn towards the Eternal, that no transitory thing may move him, no corporeal thing affect him, no earthly thing attract him. This was the meaning of St Paul when he said, "I live; yet not I; Christ liveth in me."

Now the question arises what is sanctification, since it has so lofty a rank. Thou shouldest know that real sanctification consists in this that the spirit remain as immovable and unaffected by all impact of love or hate, joy or sorrow, honour or shame, as a huge mountain is unstirred by a gentle breeze. This immovable sanctification causes man to attain the nearest likeness to God that he is capable of. God's very essence consists of His immovable sanctity; thence springs His glory and unity and impassibility. If a man is to become as like God as a creature may, that must be by sanctification. It is this which draws men upward to glory, and from glory to unity, and from unity to impassibility, and effects a resemblance between God and men.

The chief agent in this is grace, because grace draws men from the transitory and purifies them from the earthly. And thou shouldest know that to be empty of all creature's love is to be full of God, and to be full of creature-love is to be empty of God.

God has remained from everlasting in immovable sanctity, and still remains so. When He created heaven and earth and all creatures, His sanctity was as little affected thereby as though He had created nothing. I say further: God's sanctity is as little affected by men's good works and prayers, as though they had accomplished none, and He is by those means no more favourably inclined towards men than if they ceased praying and working. I say even more: when the Divine Son became man and suffered that affected the sanctity of God as little as though He had never become man at all.

Here some one may make the objection: "Are then all good works and prayers thrown away, since God is unmoved by them, and at the same time we are told to pray to Him for everything?" In answer to this I say that God from all eternity saw everything that would happen, and also when, and how He would make all creatures: He foresaw also all the prayers which would be offered, and which of them He would hear: He saw the earnest prayers which thou wilt offer tomorrow, but He will not listen to them tomorrow, because He heard them in eternity, before thou wast a man at all. If, however, thy prayer is half-hearted and not in earnest, God will not deny it now, seeing that He has denied it in eternity. Thus God remains always in His immovable sanctity, but sincere prayer and good works are not lost, for whoso doeth well, will be well rewarded.

When God appears to be angry or to do us a kindness, it is we who are altered, while He remains unchangeable, as the same sunshine is injurious to weak eyes and beneficial to strong ones, remaining in itself the same. Regarding this Isidorus in his book concerning the highest good says, "People ask what was God doing before He created heaven and earth, or whence came the new desire in God to create?" To this he answers, "No new desire arose in God, seeing that creation was everlastingly present in Him, and in His intelligence." Moses said to God, "When Pharaoh asks me who Thou art, what shall I answer?" God said, "Say, I AM hath sent me unto you," that is to say, "He Who is unchangeable hath sent me."

Perhaps some one may ask, "Was Christ

then also unchangeable, when He said, 'My soul is troubled even unto death,' or Mary when she stood under the Cross and lamented?" Here, thou shouldest know that in every man are two kinds of men, the outer and the inner man. Every man, who loves God, only uses his outer senses so far as is absolutely necessary; he takes care that they do not drag him down to the level of the beasts, as they do some who might rather he termed beasts than men. The soul of the spiritual man whom God moves to love Him with all his powers concentrates all its forces on the inner man. Therefore He saith, "Thou shalt love the Lord thy God with all thy heart." Now, there are some who waste the powers of the soul for the use of the outer man; these are they who turn all their thoughts and desires towards transitory things, and know nothing of the inner life. But a good man sometimes deprives his outer man of all power that it may have a higher object, while sensualists deprive the inner man of all power to use it for the outer man.

The outer man may go through various experiences, while the inner man is quite free and immovable. Now both in Christ and in Our Lady there was an inner and an outer man; when they spoke of outward things, they did so with the outward man, while the inner man remained immovable.

It may be asked: "What is the object of this immovable sanctity?" I answer, "Nothing": that is, so far as God has His way with a man, for He has not His way with all men.

Although God is Almighty, He can only work in a heart when He finds readiness or makes it. He works differently in men than in stones. For this we may take the following illustration: if we bake in one oven three loaves of barley-bread, of rye-bread, and of wheat, we shall find the same heat of the oven affects them differently; when one is well-baked, another will be still raw, and another yet more raw. That is not due to the heat, but to the variety of the materials. Similarly God works in all hearts not alike but in proportion as He finds them prepared and susceptible. If the heart is to be ready for the highest, it must he vacant of all other things. If I wish to write on a white tablet, whatever else is written on the tablet, however noble its purport, is a hindrance to me. If I am to write, I must wipe the tablet clean of everything, and the tablet is most suitable for my purpose when it is blank. Similarly, if God is to write on my heart, everything else must come out of it till it is really sanctified. Only so can God work

His highest will, and so the sanctified heart has no outward object at all.

The question arises: But what then does the sanctified heart pray for? I answer that when truly sanctified, it prays for nothing, for whosoever prays asks God to give him some good, or to take some evil from him. But the sanctified heart desires nothing, and contains nothing that it wishes to be freed from. Therefore it is free of all want except that it wants to be like God. St Dionysius commenting on the text, "Know ye not that all run, but one receiveth the prize?" says "this running is nothing else than a turning away from all creatures and being united to the Uncreated." When the soul gets to this point, it loses its own distinctiveness, and vanishes in God as the crimson of sunrise disappears in the sun. To this goal only pure sanctification can arrive.

St Augustine says. "the strong attraction of the soul to the Divine reduces everything to nothingness: on earth this attraction is manifested as sanctification. When this process has reached its culminating point, knowledge becomes ignorance, desire indifference and light darkness. The reason why God desires a sanctified heart more than any other is apparent when we ask the question, "What does God seek in all things?" The mouth of Wisdom says to us, "In all things I seek rest," and rest is to be found only in the sanctified heart; therein therefore God is more glad to dwell than in any other thing.

Thou shouldest also know that the more a man sets himself to be receptive of divine influence, the happier he is: who most sets himself so, is the happiest. Now no man can reach this condition of receptivity except by conformity with God, which comes from submission to God. This is what Saint Paul means when he says, "Put on the Lord Jesus Christ," that is "be conformed to Christ." Whosoever wishes to comprehend the lofty rank and benefit of sanctification must mark Christ's words to His disciples regarding His humanity, "It is profitable for you, that I go away, for, if I go not away, the Comforter will not come to you." As if to say, "Ye have so much desire towards my natural outward form, that ye cannot fully desire the Holy Spirit." Therefore put away forms and unite yourselves with formless Being, for God's spiritual comfort is only offered to those who despise earthly comfort.

Now, all thoughtful folk, mark me! no one can be truly happy, except he who abides in the strictest sanctification. No bodily and

fleshly delight can ever take place with out
spiritual loss, for the flesh lusteth against
the spirit, and the spirit against the flesh.
Therefore, the more a man fleeth from the
created, the more the Creator hastens to him.
And consider this: if the pleasure we take in
the outward image of our Lord Jesus Christ
diminishes our capacity for receiving the
Holy Spirit, how much more must our unbri-
dled desire for earthly comforts diminish it!

Therefore sanctification is the best of all
things, for it cleanses the soul, and illumi-
nates the conscience, and kindles the heart,
and wakens the spirit, and girds up the loins,
and glorifies virtue and separates us from
creatures, and unites us with God. The quick-
est means to bring us to perfection is suffering; none enjoy everlasting blessedness more
than those who share with Christ the bitter-
est pangs. Nothing is sharper than suffering,
nothing is sweeter than to have suffered. The
surest foundation in which this perfection
may rest is humility; whatever here crawls
in the deepest abjectness, that the Spirit lifts
to the very heights of God, for love brings
suffering and suffering brings love. Ways of
living are many; one lives thus, and another
thus; but whosoever will reach the highest
life, let him in a few words hear the conclu-

sion of the whole matter: keep thyself clear of all men, keep thyself from all imaginations that crowd upon the mind, free thyself from all that is contingent, entangling, and cumbersome and direct thy mind always to gazing upon God in thy heart with a steadfast look that never wavers: as for other spiritual exercises —fasting, watching and prayer — direct them all to this one end, and practice them so far as they may be helpful thereto, so wilt thou win to perfection. Here some one may ask, "Who can thus gaze always without wavering at a divine object?" I answer: "No one who now lives." This has only been said to thee that thou mightest know what the highest is, and that thou mightest have desires after it. But when thou losest sight of the Divine, thou shouldest feel as if bereft of thine eternal salvation, and shouldest long to recover it, and watch over thyself at all times, and direct thy aims and longing towards it. May God be blessed for ever. Amen.

God is at home, it's we who have gone out for a walk.
- Meister Eckhart

Truly, it is in darkness that one finds the light, so when we are in sorrow, then this

light is nearest of all to us.
- Meister Eckhart

Outward and Inward Morality

I Cor. xv. 10.—"The Grace of God."

GRACE is from God, and works in the depth of the soul whose powers it employs. It is a light which issues forth to do service under the guidance of the Spirit. The Divine Light permeates the soul, and lifts it above the turmoil of temporal things to rest in God. The soul cannot progress except with the light which God has given it as a nuptial gift; love works the likeness of God into the soul. The peace, freedom and blessedness of all souls consist in their abiding in God's will. Towards this union with God for which it is created the soul strives perpetually. Fire converts wood into its own likeness, and the stronger the wind blows, the greater grows the fire. Now by the fire understand love, and by the wind the Holy Spirit. The stronger the influence of the Holy Spirit, the brighter grows the fire of love; but not all at once, rather gradually as the soul grows. Light causes flowers and plants to grow and bear fruit; in animals it produces life, but in men blessedness. This comes from the grace of God, Who uplifts the soul, for if the soul is to grow God-like it must be lifted above itself.

To produce real moral freedom, God's grace and man's will must co-operate. As God is the Prime Mover of nature, so also He creates free impulses towards Himself and to all good things. Grace renders the will free that it may do everything with God's help, working with grace as with an instrument which belongs to it. So the will arrives at freedom through love, nay, becomes itself love, for love unites with God. All true morality, inward and outward, is comprehended in love, for love is the foundation of all the commandments.

All outward morality must be built upon this basis, not on self-interest. As long as man loves something else than God, or outside God, he is not free, because he has not love. Therefore there is no inner freedom which does not manifest itself in works of love. True freedom is the government of nature in and outside man through God; freedom is essential existence unaffected by creatures. But love often begins with fear; fear is the approach to love: fear is like the awl which draws the shoemaker's thread through the leather.

As for outward works they are ordained

for this purpose that the outward man may be directed to God. But the inner work, the work of God in the soul is the chief matter; when a man finds this within himself, he can let go externals. No law is given to the righteous, because he fulfils the law inwardly, and bears it in himself, for the least thing done by God is better than all the work of creatures. But this is intended for those who are enlightened by God and the Holy Scriptures.

But here on earth man never attains to being unaffected by external things. There never was a Saint so great as to be immovable. I can never arrive at a state when discord shall be as pleasing to my ears as harmony. Some people wish to do without good works. I say, "This cannot be." As soon as the disciples received the Holy Ghost, they began to work. When Mary sat at the feet of our Lord that was her school time. But afterwards when Christ went to heaven, and she received the Holy Spirit, she began to serve and was a handmaid of the disciples. When saints become saints, they begin to work, and so gather to the refuge of everlasting safety.

How can a man abide in love, when he does not keep God's commands which issue forth from love? How can the inner man be born in God, when the outer man abides not in the following of Christ, in self-mortification and in suffering, for there is no being born of God, except through Christ. Love is the fulfilling of all commands; therefore however much man strives to reach this freedom, the body can never quite attain thereto, and must be ever in conflict. Seeing that good works are the witness of the Holy Ghost, man can never do without them. The aim of man is not outward holiness by works, but life in God, yet this last expresses itself in works of love.

Outward as well as inward morality helps to form the idea of true Christian freedom. We are right to lay stress on inwardness, but in this world there is no inwardness without an outward expression. If we regard the soul as the formative principle of the body, and God as the formative principle of the soul, we have a profounder principle of ethics than is found in Pantheism. The fundamental thought of this system is the real distinction between God and the world, together with their real inseparability, for only really distinct elements can interpenetrate each other.

The inner work is first of all the work of God's grace in the depth of the soul which subsequently distributes itself among the faculties of the soul, in that of Reason appearing as Belief, in that of Will as Love, and in that of Desire as Hope. When the Divine Light penetrates the soul, it is united with God as light with light. This is the light of faith. Faith bears the soul to heights unreachable by her natural senses and faculties.

As the peculiar faculty of the eye is to see form and colour, and of the ear to hear sweet tones and voices, so is aspiration peculiar to the soul. To relax from ceaseless aspiration is sin. This energy of aspiration directed to and grasping God, as far as is possible for the creature, is called Hope, which is also a divine virtue. Through this faculty the soul acquires such great confidence that she deems nothing in the Divine Nature beyond her reach.

The third faculty is the inward Will, which, always turned to God like a face, absorbs to itself love from God. According to the diverse directions in which redemptive Grace through the Holy Spirit is imparted to the different faculties of men, it finds corresponding expression as one of the Spirit's seven gifts. This impartation constitutes man's spiritual birth which brings him out of sin into a state of grace while natural birth makes him a sinner.

As God can only be seen by His own light, so He can only be loved by His own love. The merely natural man is incapable of this, because nature by itself is incapable of responding to the Divine Love and is confined within its own circle. Therefore it is necessary for Grace, which is a simple supernatural power, to elevate the natural faculties to union in God above the merely temporal objects of existence. The possibility of love to God is grounded in the relative likeness between man and God. If the soul is to reach its moral goal, i.e. Godlikeness, it must become inwardly like God through grace, and a spiritual birth which is the spring of true morality. The inner work that man has to do is the practical realization of Grace: without this, all outward work is ineffectual for salvation. Virtue is never mere virtue, it is either from God, or through God, or in God. All the soul's works which are to inherit an everlasting recompense must be carried on in God. They are rewarded by Him in proportion as they are carried on in Him, for the soul is an instrument of God whereby He carries on His work.

The essence of morality is inwardness, the intensity of will from which it springs, and the nobleness of the aim for which it is practiced. When a good work is done by a man, he is free of it, and through that freedom is liker and nearer to his Original than he was before.

The moral task of man is a process of spiritualization. All creatures are go-betweens, and we are placed in time that by diligence in spiritual business we may grow liker and nearer to God. The aim of man is beyond the temporal —in the serene region of the everlasting Present.

In this sense the New Birth of man is the focus towards which all creation strives, because man is the image of God after the likeness of which the world is created. All time strives towards eternity or the timeless Now, out of which it issued at creation. The merely temporal life in itself is a negation of real being, because it depends on itself and not on the deepest foundation of life; therefore also natural love is cramped finite and defective. It must through grace be lifted to the highest sphere of existence, and attain to freedom outside the narrow confines of the natural. Thereby love becomes real love, because only that is real which is comprehended and loved in its essence. Only by grace man comes from the temporal and transitory to be one with God. This lifting of manifoldness to unity is the supreme aim of ethics; by thus the divine birth is completed on the side of man.

This passage from nothingness to real being, this quitting of oneself is a birth accompanied by pain, for by it natural love is excluded. All grief except grief for sin comes from love of the world. In God is neither sorrow, nor grief, nor trouble. Wouldst thou be free from all grief and trouble, abide and walk in God, and to God alone. As long as love of the creature is in us, pain cannot cease.

This is the chief significance of the suffering of Christ for us, that we cast all our grief into the ocean of His suffering. If thou sufferest only regarding thyself, from whatever cause it may be, that suffering causes grief to thee, and is hard to bear. But if thou sufferest regarding God and Him alone, that suffering is not grievous, nor hard to bear, because God bears the load. The love of the Cross must swallow up our personal grief. Whoso does not suffer from love, for him sorrow is sorrow and grievous to bear; but whoso suffers from love he sorrows not, and his suffering is fruitful in God. Therefore is sorrow so noble; he who sorrows most is the noblest. Now no mortal's sorrow was like the sorrow which Christ bore; therefore he is far nobler than any man. Verily were there anything nobler than sorrow, God would have redeemed man thereby. Sorrow is the root of all virtue.

Through the higher love the whole life of man is to be elevated from temporal selfishness to the spring of all love, to God: man will again be master over nature by abiding in God and lifting her up to God.

When you are thwarted, it is your own attitude that is out of order.
- Meister Eckhart

What a man takes in by contemplation, that he pours out in love.
- Meister Eckhart

To be full of things is to be empty of God.
To be empty of things is to be full of God.
- Meister Eckhart

The outward man is the swinging door;
the inner man is the still hinge.
- Meister Eckhart

Words derive their power from the original word.
- Meister Eckhart

*The outward work will never be puny if the
inward work is great.*
- Meister Eckhart

*What we plant in the soil of contemplation,
we shall reap in the harvest of action.*
- Meister Eckhart

*If the only prayer you ever say in your entire
life is thank you,
it will be enough.*
- Meister Eckhart

*One person who has mastered life is better
than a thousand
persons who have mastered only the contents
of books,
but no one can get anything out of life without God.*
- Meister Eckhart

*God expects but one thing of you, and that
is that
you should come out of yourself in so
far as you are
a created being made and let God be God
in you.*
- Meister Eckhart

*Do exactly what you would do if you felt
most secure.
- Meister Eckhart*

*The more we have the less we own.
- Meister Eckhart*

*We are celebrating the feast of the Eternal
Birth which
God the Father has borne and never ceases
to bear in all eternity...
But if it takes not place in me, what avails
it? Everything lies in this,
that it should take place in me.
- Meister Eckhart*

*There exists only the present instant...
a Now which always and without
end i s i tself new.
There is no yesterday nor any tomorrow,
but only Now, as i t was a thousand
years ago and as
it will be a thousand years hence.
- Meister Eckhart*

*A human being has so many skins inside,
covering the depths of the heart.
We know so many things, but we don't
know ourselves!*

*Why, thirty or forty skins or hides,
as thick and hard as an ox's or bear's,
cover the soul.
Go into your own ground and learn to
know yourself there.*
- Meister Eckhart

*In whatever way you find God most, and
you are most aware of God, that is the way
you should follow. But if another way pres-
ents itself, quite contrary to the first, and if,
having abandoned the first way, you find
God as much in the new way as in the one
you left, then that is right. But, the noblest
and best thing would be this: if a person
were to come to such equality, with such
calm and certainty that one could find and
enjoy God in any way and in all things,
without having to wait for anything or chase
after anything: that would delight me!...
Every work helps towards this. If anything
does not help towards this, you should let
it go ("The Master's Final Words", vol. 3,
Meister Eckhart, ed. O'C. Walshe).*